How To Be Happy

HOW
TO BE
HAPPY

Lama Zopa Rinpoche

Edited by Josh Bartok and Ailsa Cameron

Wisdom Publications · Boston

WISDOM PUBLICATIONS
199 Elm Street
Somerville MA 02144 USA
www.wisdompubs.org
617-776-7416

*Library of Congress
Cataloging-in-Publication Data*
Thubten Zopa, Rinpoche, 1945–
 How to be happy / Lama Zopa Rin-
poche ; edited by Josh Bartok and Ailsa
Cameron.
  p. cm.
 ISBN 0-86171-196-3 (hardcover : alk.
paper)
1. Religious life—Buddhism. I. Bartok,
Josh. II. Cameron, Ailsa. III. Title.
 BQ7775.T79 2008
 294.3'444—dc22

2008015537

12 11 10 09 08
5 4 3 2 1

Cover and interior design by
Gopa & Ted2, Inc. Set in Village 9.8/18.
Photo of Lama Zopa © 2008 Roger Kunsang.
Cover illustration by Lama Zopa Rinposhe.

Publisher's Acknowledgment

The publisher gratefully acknowledges the
generous help of the Hershey Family
Foundation in sponsoring the production
of this book.

Table of Contents

Meditations

Lama Zopa Rinpoche

Happiness

EVERY ONE OF US WANTS HAPPINESS, and not only in each moment of our daily life: we want an unchanging, ultimate happiness that can be experienced forever.

Every one of us is trying to stop our problems and find peace. No matter where we live, what race or culture we belong to, what religion or philosophy we follow, or what language we speak, we all wish to be happy and not have problems. Truly every living being has the basic wish to experience happiness and avoid suffering.

But so often, our attempts to find happiness end up only causing more pain.

We need to understand the full potential of our mind, and we need to understand the importance of loving-kindness for our own happiness and for the happiness of the world. We need to learn how to transform our daily work so that it becomes the cause of happiness rather than problems, now and in the future. And we need to learn how to transform every single experience—health and sickness, wealth and poverty, living and dying—into happiness. Meditation is the most powerful tool we can employ to do this. Through the power of meditation, we can find lasting peace and happiness and, more importantly, we can bring peace and happiness to others.

Cultivate the thought that everyone you meet—in all circumstances—is fulfilling all your wishes.
This is the gate to true happiness.

The sun of real happiness shines in your life only when you start to cherish others.

PROBLEMS AND THE ABSENCE of problems do not come from outside. Problems and the absence of problems, as well as all peace and all happiness, only come from your own mind. Your mind has the potential to stop the problems that come from your mind. And yet the same mind that brings the problem doesn't stop the problem, but another mind—another thought, another attitude—can stop all problems and bring peace and happiness.

The mind of a buddha or some holy being can't be transplanted into you. Peace, happiness, and satisfaction have to come from your own mind.

AS LONG AS WE BELIEVE that happiness has to come from outside, from other people or from the external environment, we will always blame something outside whenever we have a problem. Many people, for example, think that their problems come from their parents. They say, "I'm like this because of my mother and father. My parents are to blame." In a way, Western culture as a whole teaches children to blame their parents for their problems, rather than emphasizing how kind parents are in giving life to their children. But real happiness has nothing to do with the past, with our history, or our upbringing. Real happiness comes when we free ourselves from the dissatisfied mind of desire. Satisfaction comes when we give ourselves freedom from the always unhappy mind of desire.

**Suffering is the broom that
clears away negative karma.**

THE HAPPINESS OF MATERIAL progress
is artificial, just some kind of external excite-
ment—the briefest flash of lightning in the dark.
True joy, lasting joy, comes from the depths of
the heart.

**Renounce the happiness that produces suffering;
cherish the true happiness that
can come from suffering.**

Meditation

YOU CANNOT MAKE your body flexible just by thinking about making it flexible. You can only do that by training it; the *body* has to make the body flexible. Just as physical flexibility has to be created by our body, mental flexibility—which is another name for ultimate peace and happiness—has to be created by our mind, through mental training.

Meditation is mental training.

MEDITATION is a profound psychological technique to stop wrong conceptions and to start the correct way of thinking that leads to peace, happiness, and harmony. Meditation sounds like some kind of religious term, but it is actually the deepest practice of inner psychology. Meditation protects the mind, and keeps it aware of reality. Meditation also helps you keep your mind in a state of loving-kindness by training you to be aware of all the ways in which others are kind to you; and it helps you maintain compassion by being aware of how others are suffering.

How do we fill up the emptiness in our heart? The answer is meditation.

TO TAKE UP REAL MEDITATION, real spiritual practice, is to transform suffering into happiness—and that depends on transforming your mind, your attitude.

YOU HAVE TO WORK to gradually develop your mind from day to day, and year to year. It might even take eons. Ultimately this kind of mind-training is a practice of patience.

CERTAIN KINDS OF MEDITATION practices are like destroying the root of a poisonous plant so that it cannot produce seeds and grow again and again, causing a lot of harm: you destroy the root of suffering-causing karma so that that seed cannot grow to produce problems.

A MEDITATION TEACHER is part of an emergency rescue operation, like when police, paramedics, and rescue workers go in with sirens blaring, red and blue lights flashing, helicopters whirling overhead with searchlights— to help people drowning in danger and distress.

THE DHARMA ITSELF is like a life-jacket. But it's up to you to wear the life-jacket as you cross the perilous sea of suffering; it's up to you to practice.

MEDITATION is the way to make your mind calm, clear, and stable; it is the way to stop creating harm. Meditation is the way to have peace; ultimately it is the way to stop creating problems. But just to have peace of mind yourself is not sufficient. The most important purpose of practicing meditation is to develop the good heart, *bodhichitta*—the aspiration to give others less harm and more benefit. But even though you might not have yet developed your mind to the point where you have completely stopped harming others and only benefit them, you should still strive to cultivate *bodhichitta*.

ALWAYS STRIVE to improve your mind, improve your attitude. Rather than using your intelligence and the vast potential you have as a human being to create more problems for yourself and for the world, cultivate the good heart, *bodhichitta,* and cultivate wisdom. Train your mind to become less and less angry and more patient, less selfish and more loving, more compassionate and more concerned with the happiness of others. Without actively working to do this, however, your mind will remain just the same, or more likely become even worse, building up more anger, more pride, more desire, more dissatisfaction. This is how all violence happens.

**Wisdom simply means
awareness of reality.**

LIKE BOILING WATER, our mind is bubbling with superstitions, hallucinations, and many unnecessary and wrong views, which bring only harm and no peace in our life.

By learning methods to pacify our disturbing thoughts, to cool our boiling mind, we are taking the opportunity to free ourselves from the causes of problems and unhappiness.

Meditation is the unfailing way to get free from problems.

WHEN ANY OF THE FIVE DELUSIONS arise—ignorance, anger, attachment, jealousy, miserliness—look at them as completely pure minds of wisdom. When strong desire arises, just concentrate on the nature of desire, thinking that it is the transcendental wisdom of discernment of a buddha's pure holy mind, a manifestation of the *dharmakaya,* ultimately pure in nature. When you look at the pure nature of any delusion, the delusion is stopped. When you meditate like this, even for a moment, the five delusions disappear, and you also leave a positive imprint on your consciousness, which can ripen into that transcendental wisdom.

SUBDUING YOUR OWN MIND is the essence of the Buddha's teaching—and the basic method for subduing the mind is meditation. Yet even though we can accomplish so many other things in our life, we find it very hard to develop our mind. When a problem comes, our mind reacts the same way it did before we learned anything about meditation—our mind becomes disturbed, and we are dissatisfied and angry. This happens because we haven't done the real practice of watching and, most importantly, working to subdue our mind. If subduing our mind had been our main practice, our mind would definitely have developed year by year, month by month, week by week, and even day by day. With the necessary causes and conditions—diligent practice of meditation, of mind-training—the mind surely develops. Please see for yourself!

Right now, why not take the opportunity to enjoy your life with the Dharma?

THE ULTIMATE GOAL OF MEDITATING, of practicing Dharma, is to bring happiness to every living being, now and continuingly into the future. Our aim is to bring all beings happiness until we and they together end the cycle of death and rebirth into problems and suffering.

Desire

WHEN YOUR MIND IS OVERWHELMED by strong desire, it interferes with your seeing reality clearly. Desire clings to the exaggerated appearance of the object of desire as permanently, truly, self-existently *good*. After you exaggerate the good qualities of the object and label it "good," you hallucinate that it appears as something good from its own side—and you then cling to that. Clinging to that exaggerated appearance interferes with the ability to see the ultimate nature of the object.

When this happens, rather than looking at the *object*, the person or thing you desire, you should look at the *subject*, your mind. Simply watch your mind. Change the object of attention from outside (the thing you are hallucinating about) to inside (the hallucinating mind itself). Instead of thinking of that external object, look at the mind that is thinking of that object. When you practice even this simple meditation there's immediately a change. Overpowering desire suddenly has the potential to be stopped. There's space in your mind to see the true nature of yourself and of the object of your desire. If you do this even for a moment, the desiring mind starts to become controlled, pacified, subdued.

The dissatisfied mind of desire is one of the main causes of stress.

**Letting go of attachment is not a loss;
you are not losing anything.
Truly, when you let go of suffering you
gain inner peace and deep satisfaction.**

You FOLLOW DESIRE WITH THE AIM of getting satisfaction. Your aim is worthwhile and you are right to wish to obtain it—but the method is wrong and results only in dissatisfaction.

Following desire cannot lead to satisfaction.

You FOLLOW DESIRE and you are not satisfied. Again you follow desire, and again you are not satisfied. Again you try, and again you are not satisfied.

**Clinging to a small pleasure becomes
an obstacle to obtaining the great pleasure
of ultimate happiness.**

WHEN I SAY that you should give up desire,
it might sound as if I'm telling you to give up
your happiness—but this isn't so! If you ever
really look deeply at desire and the objects of
desire, you will see that even though such
things appear as pleasures, there is no real
pleasure to be found there. Cutting off desire,
however, doesn't mean that you cut off all happiness—far from it! Truly, when you renounce
desire you open yourself in the only way possible to true happiness. Because you may not
have experienced this true happiness yet, you
mistake the subtle suffering of desire for true
peace—but once you realize the infinite

benefits of renouncing selfishness and desire, this kind of renunciation is a joyful act.

Attachment is like honey on a razor's edge: it looks like pleasure but offers only pain.

OFTEN, BEFORE THE BENEFITS of renouncing desire have completely become clear to you, it's as if there are two warring parties in your mind: the party of desire and the party of wisdom. You have to take the side of one of them. Rather than taking the side of desire, choose to take the side of Dharma wisdom. This simple act is like choosing reality over hallucination.

Any samsaric pleasure is nothing new, only more suffering.

SAMSARIC PLEASURE, which is dependent on external things, is only suffering. When one problem stops and another problem has started but is still small, we call it "pleasure." We project the appearance of pleasure and believe in that. And in this way we see the unbearable prison of samsara as a lush, beautiful park—which is, after all, a hallucination.

As long as you follow desire
you will never find satisfaction.

Attitude ·

DIFFICULT EMOTIONS OR MEMORIES are only problems if you don't have methods to transform them. If you don't remember or don't apply those methods of thought-transformation, difficult emotions and memories bring only suffering. However, if you apply the right tools, the tools of thought-transformation, the more these things appear to you, the more practice you can do! Isn't that wonderful?

It is truly possible to transform your whole life and your whole mind into the essence of Dharma itself.

WHENEVER YOU EXPERIENCE a problem, think: "I am experiencing this problem on behalf of all other beings. Instead of allowing countless other people to experience it, I alone will take all these problems upon myself, so that everyone else can be free of them." This attitude stops the problem by purifying the cause of the problem, which is always within your mind. Experiencing your problems in this way keeps your mind happy and benefits others—and when your problem benefits others, it also, of course, benefits you.

Everything depends on how you use your mind.

WHENEVER YOU ARE at your lowest—when you are most depressed, when your partner has left you, when you've lost your job—that is the time to fight your true enemy: delusion. Think to yourself: "Now is the time to do battle, to go to war with the samsaric emotions. Samsara has never brought any real happiness and now is the time for me to realize this." When you do this, you're making war with your inner enemy; you are taking steps to conquer the enemy that has defeated you for endless samsaric rebirths, from time without beginning. All other seeming enemies cannot last long once the inner enemy has fallen.

Cherishing yourself is the door to all obstacles. Selflessly cherishing others, even one other being, is the door to all happiness.

SINCE WE EXPERIENCE SICKNESS, why not experience sickness with the thought to benefit others?

Since we experience loss, why not experience loss with the thought to benefit others?

Since we experience hardships, why not experience hardships with the thought to benefit others?

Since we experience relationship problems, why not do so with the thought to benefit others?

Since we must experience death, why not experience even death with the thought to benefit others?

What life could be happier or more meaningful than this?

WHEN YOU EXPERIENCE any negative state—even depression—*for others,* for the numberless beings suffering everywhere, it becomes the path for you to achieve enlightenment. Even depression can be a wish-granting jewel, the most precious one of all, fulfilling your own wishes for happiness and those of all beings.

Transform all undesirable conditions by voluntarily taking up all difficulties.

PEOPLE CAN'T SEE YOUR MIND, what people see is a manifestation of your attitude in your actions of body and speech. Practice with the bodhisattva attitude every day; let your actions of body and speech express your aspiration to bring ultimate happiness to all beings.

Don't get disturbed if you hear of problems—our ears are made to hear problems. Problems are like earrings—just decorations for the ear!

EVEN IF WE HEAR EVERY TEACHING taught by all the buddhas throughout space and time, as long as we don't change our attitude, even this won't help us to generate realizations in our mind. If we don't change our attitude, we will never be truly happy, we will never be free. This is why, even though there are numberless buddhas and bodhisattvas working tirelessly, ceaselessly, constantly, so many beings are still suffering. It's not because the holy beings are not helping us; it's because from our side we haven't attempted to change our attitude.

If it were only in the hands of the buddhas and bodhisattvas (or in the hands of God, for that matter), there wouldn't be any beings suffering now. But in fact, being free from suffering is dependent upon both us *and* the holy beings.

The buddhas and bodhisattvas are like doctors, and their teaching is like medicine. And just as with physical illness, even if we have an excellent doctor who knows all about our disease and its treatment and can definitely cure us, we won't recover from our illness if we don't take it upon ourselves to follow her advice. If we don't recover and we haven't followed the doctor's advice, it's not the doctor's fault! If we won't listen to the doctor when we are sick, what can the doctor do? Nothing.

It's very important to understand and to remember this point.

The way to solve the problems in your life is to open your heart to others.

No matter how many or difficult are the hardships, by receiving them for others we transform our life.

A PERSON'S DEVELOPMENT OF MIND can affect the environment; it can transform the environment.

Take my teacher, Lama Yeshe, for example. Lama Yeshe saw everyone as very kind. In my observation, because of Lama's own good heart, other people around him also became kind and good-hearted. Being around Lama transformed the other person's mind or, we might say, *blessed* the other person's mind. This means that other mind was transformed from having a negative attitude to a positive one, from a selfish mind into a kind mind.

You need to guard your attitude all the time, twenty-four hours a day. Doing only what your mind says, believing everything your mind says, is very dangerous—it's usually what the delusions want, not what the bodhisattva wants.

**Don't underestimate
the power of attitude!**

Peace

WHEN YOU GET UP IN THE MORNING, think of the meaning of your human life, think of your universal responsibility: "I'm responsible for all beings. I will act to pacify all their suffering and bring them happiness." As you dress, think: "I'm putting on these clothes because I need to fulfill my universal responsibility." When you are eating, again remember the meaning, the purpose, of this precious human life. Think of your food as medicine to keep you strong in order for you to better serve all beings. When you go to sleep, again remember the meaning of this human life. Sleep too is like medicine—you are going to sleep to become refreshed so that tomorrow you can again work diligently to fulfill your universal responsibility. Do all your activities for others. Eat for others, sleep for others, work for others, live for others. And when it comes time to die, even do this for others.

This is a real, practical contribution to world peace that you can make at any time, day and night.

Your own loving-kindness provides happiness to all living beings.

ALL PEACE AND ALL HAPPINESS—of families, societies, countries—depends on each of us having loving-kindness toward each other.

EACH OF US is completely responsible for the happiness of every other being. Each of us has this universal responsibility. It's completely up to us. When you work with your mind, what you are doing is the real, ultimate solution for world peace—and not only peace on earth, but for all the beings in all the numberless universes.

The circumstantial, temporary absence of war is not real peace. Real peace comes only from the heart.

WE MIGHT HAVE BIG IDEAS about how we can contribute to world peace, but if we can't help bring peace in our own family, our own workplace—even our own mind—how can we ever start?

Compassion

Live with compassion.
Work with compassion.
Die with compassion.
Meditate with compassion.
Enjoy with compassion.

When problems come,
Experience them with compassion.

SHAKYAMUNI BUDDHA, when he was still a bodhisattva, made charity of his holy body for three countless great eons. To those people who needed eyes, he gave his eyes; to those who needed limbs, he gave his limbs; and in one life he gave his whole holy body to a family of starving tigers. He also became a king many times and repeatedly made charity of all his wealth to the poor. For three countless great eons, Shakyamuni Buddha practiced the six perfections: charity, patience, morality, perseverance, concentration, and wisdom. He then achieved enlightenment for us and for all beings, in order to free us all from all suffering and lead us all to enlightenment.

Let us also strive to live our lives like this, let us strive to repay that kindness.

**Compassion is a wish-granting jewel,
fulfilling all our ultimate desires.**

WHEN WE FEEL COMPASSION for a person or an animal—any being at all—we wish that being to be free from suffering. When our compassion is strong, we don't simply *wish* for this but actually *do* something about it. We ourselves take responsibility for freeing that being from suffering.

In this way, each of us is completely responsible for pacifying all the sufferings of all beings and for bringing them happiness. It is completely in our hands. Each of us has this universal responsibility.

In every interaction: be careful, be kind.

Compassion is the first thing to remember, the first thing to practice.

PAY CLOSE ATTENTION to your behavior toward other people. You may not always feel compassion for everyone, but you do have some compassion. Rejoice in even this.

Practice compassion even if no one else does.

· Compassion for the Enemy ·

There is no harm to oneself that doesn't come from one's own mind.

HOW CAN YOU DEVELOP COMPASSION for someone who hates you?

First of all, you have to see that the person is completely overwhelmed by ignorance, anger, and the dissatisfied mind of desire. It is important to immediately recall that the person has no freedom at all, but is completely overwhelmed, almost possessed, by delusions—just as Tibet was overwhelmed and possessed by the Chinese. The person who hates you is surely overwhelmed by not just one delusion, but many.

Rather than thinking that the person is the *same as* their anger, is *one with* their anger—which is not the reality—you have to see that the person and their delusion, their anger, are separate. Even if the person hallucinates they are one with their anger, they are not. What's more, thinking that they are one with their anger—rather than sufferingly afflicted by it themselves—will only make you more upset. Whereas, if you think that the person and their anger are different, as they are indeed different in reality, then there is some space in your mind for compassion to arise.

Even if this person who hates you experiences pleasure in hating you, their pleasure is really suffering that is just appearing as pleasure. The person who hates you may call their hatred "pleasure," but it is still only suffering. It is just a question of whether the person notices that. This is the second reason why the person who hates you is an object of compassion.

The third reason is that he or she, just like you, also experiences "the suffering of suffering"—which means rebirth, old age, sickness, death, meeting undesirable objects, separating from desirable ones, and all the other countless problems of life. How painful for that person!

On top of all these sufferings, out of delusion the person who hates you creates the karma to suffer *yet more*—to be born yet again into the suffering realms.

And then, if you do not practice patience in response to that anger, do not cultivate compassion for this suffering being, and instead return anger to that person, by requiting that anger, you are pushing that suffering being toward *still more* harming karma. You are throwing him or her over the precipice into the unimaginable suffering of the lower realms.

When you reflect on all this, there is no real choice: you have to feel compassion for each person—even for the one who appears to you as an enemy!

If an action harms any other being, even your enemy, it harms you.

WHEN SOMEONE DISLIKES YOU or treats you bitterly, when someone appears to you as an enemy, you have the wonderful opportunity to practice patience and in that way develop your mind in the path of wisdom and compassion. Without the existence of someone who shows anger or dislike toward you, you have no such opportunity. If this person loved you, if this person only treated you just the way you want to be treated all the time, you would have no opportunity to develop patience, to cultivate a mind that cherishes others and truly brings happiness to all beings. This person who doesn't love you is the only one who allows you to practice patience and brings you all these infinite benefits. Since, as I am sure you can see, you have the utmost need of patience and also compassion, the person who is angry with you is actually being extremely kind!

Thinking of the particular kindness of your enemy, you can appreciate them from the depths of your heart.

When there is no anger inside, there is no enemy outside.

IF WE ARE ANGRY WITH SOMEONE, thinking that they have harmed us, we see them as our enemy. But if we look at that person with wisdom, we don't see an enemy but a very good friend working very hard to teach us patience. If we have anger, we find countless external enemies. If we don't have anger within us, we don't find even one external enemy—not if someone is criticizing us, not if someone is harming us, not even if someone is killing us!

Even someone who hates you is an object of compassion.

JUST RECOGNIZING HOW MUCH and in how many ways any being is suffering—even one who appears as your enemy—causes compassion to arise. And when it does, you should elaborate on this compassion for your enemy by thinking in a similar way about all the people in your town or city and then all the people in the whole world. Generate compassion for all of them. The nature of their suffering, of their delusions, of their hallucinations, is the same. Each one is completely trapped in their own prison. Feeling that their situation is unbearable, you want to do something for them. After all, you wouldn't feel comfortable if you didn't do something for them. Isn't that so?

The Good Heart

Think big. This is the bodhisattva's skillful means to benefit all beings everywhere.

PACIFYING YOUR OWN PROBLEMS and obtaining peace for yourself alone is not sufficient. That is, to be honest, a very small purpose for living your life. A much more worthy purpose, a purpose that leads to much more happiness for both you and all beings, is to cherish all other beings—all beings everywhere who are suffering and want happiness—the very same way that you cherish yourself. This is what brings real happiness and satisfaction.

After all, you are just one being. No matter how hard you work for yourself, it's still just one person working for one person, one person to receive any benefit. That's very limited. That attitude is very small-minded. And, since your aim—to obtain happiness only for yourself—is limited, the benefit you gain from that work is also limited. With such a limited motivation, you can't achieve the greatest benefit, ultimate happiness—and not even any real measure of temporary happiness.

Yet as soon as you start to transform your mind from cherishing yourself above all others into cherishing others even more than you cherish yourself, immediately real happiness and satisfaction becomes possible.

What if all happiness anywhere is your happiness?

IF YOU LIVE BY cherishing others, when you die you can die with a smile on your lips and a smile in your heart.

You cut the root of your problems in every moment when you cherish others.

EVEN IF YOU ARE BORN IN HELL, it's nothing much to be depressed about, because you are just one person. Even if you achieve liberation from samsara, ultimate liberation for yourself, it's nothing much to be excited about, because you are just one person. Since other beings are numberless, they are far more precious and important.

Remember that your life is for others.

EVEN FOR OUR OWN HAPPINESS, even for our own survival, compassion is the most important factor. It is the most precious thing, more precious than all the wealth in the world. The good heart is more important than friends, lovers, wealth, fame, or anything else. Practicing the good heart is more important than all other forms of education. Practicing the good heart is the most important form of meditation.

The good heart makes your whole life beneficial.

Enlightenment

RIGHT NOW, WITH THIS VERY MIND and in this very moment, you have the potential for all temporary and ultimate happiness, even up to the peerless happiness of full enlightenment.

**Without the good heart,
it is not possible to get enlightened.**

CONVENTIONALLY there is me and you, samsara and enlightenment, suffering and happiness—but in emptiness there is no difference at all. There is one taste in emptiness.

WHEN THE SUN RISES, even though there's only one sun, it is reflected in every bit of water on this earth, from tiny drops of dew on a leaf to all the great oceans, lakes, and seas. The sun doesn't have any motivation to be reflected in the water and doesn't have to put any effort into doing it. The reflections spontaneously occur as the sun rises. In a similar way, after you achieve full enlightenment, you spontaneously and perfectly guide all beings by revealing various means with your holy body, holy speech, and holy mind.

FOR THOSE WHO HAVE PURE MINDS, Buddha manifests in pure forms; for those who have impure minds, Buddha manifests in impure, or ordinary, forms. Buddha manifests as whatever is necessary to guide a particular being.

THERE MAY BE ONE BEING who maliciously tries to cut a buddha, a fully enlightened being, with a knife—and there may another being who lovingly oils and perfumes the buddha's body. But a buddha doesn't discriminate between these two beings. There is no discrimination from the side of the enlightened being—only equal compassion for both beings. A buddha doesn't feel more compassion for the person who helps and less compassion, or no compassion, for the person who cuts his body piece by piece. A buddha has no thought not to work for and help the being who harms him. A buddha works for all beings without discrimination. Let us also work toward this goal!

SHAKYAMUNI BUDDHA and all the buddhas of the past, present, and future, as well as all the great saints in various religions, were originally like us. They had ignorance, anger, desire, jealousy, pride, ill will, and all the other mental faults, as well as all the other problems in life—but they didn't just leave their life in problems. They became different from us by putting effort into developing their inner qualities, the qualities of their mind. They reduced the faults of the mind and put effort into developing the good qualities of the mind, the essence of which is compassion for all beings. Let us all do this as well.

Don't waste even a moment!

Self-Cherishing
and Cherishing Others

**Rather than taking upon yourself
all the problems you are experiencing,
give them to the ego,
the self-cherishing thought.**

REGARD THE EGO THE WAY Americans regard terrorists—how pleased they are when terrorists are harmed! Think: "My ego is trillions of times more harmful than terrorists."

**Transform every problem into
the medicine to cure the chronic disease
of self-cherishing.**

WITH EVERY PROBLEM that you can
remember ever having had, check whether it
had anything to do with your selfish mind.

If you do this diligently, no matter what the
problem is, it always eventually becomes clear
that the problem is ultimately related to self-
cherishing thought. When you investigate, you
begin to see more deeply the shortcomings of
self-cherishing thought, and you see it more as
your only true enemy.

With a perceived external enemy, the more
harmful you think that enemy is, the more distance you would work to keep between you
and him. In a similar way, the more harmful
you recognize self-cherishing thought to be, the

more distance you will naturally want to keep between you and self-cherishing thought.

ONE OTHER LIVING BEING is more precious than you. Why? Because if you cherish that being, whether a person or an animal, if you sacrifice yourself for even that being, that itself brings great purification and enables you to accumulate infinite merit. Cherishing that other being takes you to enlightenment, the perfect state of peace.

On the other hand, cherishing yourself is an obstacle to achieving enlightenment. The moment you cherish yourself you create a huge obstacle to enlightenment, a huge obstacle to your benefiting all beings by bringing them to enlightenment.

**When you cherish others,
your true success starts.**

IF WE DON'T DEVELOP OUR MINDS, if we don't transform our minds from self-cherishing thought to the thought of cherishing others, we will continuously give harm to other beings. Truly, the actions that come out of self-cherishing thought can only ever harm other beings—whether directly or indirectly. If we act with self-cherishing thought, all beings receive harm from us. It is always the case that their receiving harm is dependent upon us.

**When you cherish others,
all your wishes are fulfilled.**

THAT REAL SELF YOU HAVE BEEN projecting and cherishing, the one you have been thinking is the most precious and most important being in all the world, in reality exists nowhere, neither inside nor outside your body, neither within nor without your mind. Whenever a self-cherishing thought arises, please remember this.

Mind

**Everything depends on what you do
with your mind.**

THE MIND OF MOST OF US ORDINARY
beings is like a headstrong toddler, and needs
to be taken care of like a toddler. We can't just
do everything the mind says and give it everything it says it wants—just as we can't with a
toddler. That would lead to a very ill-mannered
child indeed! It is very dangerous to do everything the mind says.

What is the mind? It is nothing other than what is merely imputed by the mind.

MIND IS LIKE DOUGH, which means you can mold it into any shape. You can roll it into suffering, or roll it into ultimate happiness.

Mind is like a disciple, which means you must strive always to be the guru, always teaching.

Mind is like a child, which means you should become like parents, the father and mother carefully and lovingly watching the child and guiding her. If you too act like the child, believe everything the child says, if you *become* the child, you create obstacles and life becomes suffering.

Mind is a boat, and you are the captain; mind is a car and you are the driver. Learn the waters, watch the road, steer the vehicle, follow the map—letting the mind run haphazardly where it will, rudderless, captainless, driverless, is the path to great harm.

Pay attention to your attitude all the time, guard it as if you were the secret service, as if you were a bodyguard.

APPROACH YOUR MIND THE WAY a spy approaches his target. Spy on your mind. Get to know everything about it: what it is thinking, planning, acting out; whether it is working for good or causing harm—and carefully work to interfere when the mind is being negative.

THE BASIC DEFINITION OF MIND is *that which is clear and able to perceive objects.* Here, *clear* doesn't necessarily mean that the way the mind sees an object accords with reality. Here *clear* means simply seeing an object clearly, whether rightly or wrongly. For example, from a distance people in a department store might see a store mannequin as a real person. They give the label "person" to the mannequin because it has the shape of a person, and they then believe in their label. The mannequin then appears to them as a real person, even though in reality there's no actual person there. Even though that appearance is not true, it is a clear appearance to their mind.

The mind has the nature of perception; it is only to the mind that things appear.

IT IS THE CLEAR-LIGHT NATURE of the mind that gives us the potential to achieve any happiness that we wish. It is the clear-light nature of the mind that gives us every hope. It gives us the opportunity to be completely liberated from all problems, from true suffering and all causes of suffering. It is the clear-light nature of the mind that lets us achieve ultimate happiness, lets us cease even subtle obscurations.

The mind is naturally pure, inherently without faults.

THE MIND DOES NOT EXIST from its own side. The mind that appears to exist from its own side is completely empty of existing from its own side. The mind that exists is the mind that is merely imputed by the mind in dependence upon the base to be labeled mind—that phenomenon that can perceive—and on the thought that labels it. That base is not the body, but the formless phenomenon that is clear and perceives objects. In dependence upon that phenomenon, mind is merely imputed by the mind. Only in dependence upon these, the base and the thought, does the mind exist.

Each second of consciousness is also dependent on its parts.

WHEN WE HEAR ABOUT OR THINK about the mind, our mind is labeling a particular phenomenon "mind," and we then believe that there is a mind. There is no unlabeled mind. Mind is just a concept.

BECAUSE THE MIND is a dependent arising, dependent on causes and conditions,
dependent upon its base and the thought labeling it, mind is empty of existing from its own
side. This ultimate nature of the mind is
Buddha-nature, and this truth is what makes it
possible for us to achieve enlightenment.

**Even just looking at the flowers
is an expression of your mind.**

THE MIND IS LIKE A TV with many channels. On one channel all you see are problems,
problems, problems. But if you turn to another
channel, you will see everything as empty, just
labels. On the anger channel you'll see only fighting and killing. On the desire channel, there's
lust and grasping. There are so many different

programs on these two channels alone! It is important to remember that life appears to you according to your interpretation, according to the channel you choose. There's one channel where everything looks hopeless. If you change to the tantric channel, you can see everything as pure: yourself as a buddha, and the whole world as a mandala.

Everything—harmony or disharmony, a life full of problems or a life full of happiness, and even hell or enlightenment—has to do with the mind-channel you choose.

Work

PARTICULARLY AT WORK, remember the real meaning and purpose of your precious human life. Regardless of the nature of your job, as you prepare to do it think to yourself: "I'm going to offer my services to others because I wish to pacify all their suffering and bring them happiness." Even though you are paid to do your work (or even if you aren't), rather than working simply for your own happiness, think of others. Rather than going to work out of desire or selfishness, or even mere necessity, go with a positive attitude of loving-kindness, go in order to bring happiness to others. You can do this regardless of what kind of job you have.

Remember the kindness of the people who employ you. Because they have given you a job, you are able to enjoy your life, and the incredible opportunity you have to develop your mind through practicing Dharma and dedicating your efforts to others comes through their kindness.

If you work in a factory, for instance, think that the product you are making will bring comfort and happiness to the many thousands of people who will use it. If you are a teacher, think that your teaching will enable your students to find jobs, to obtain happiness, and to help others. If you are building a house, think of all the people, dogs, cats, and birds that will use the house for their comfort and protection. Remember that you are offering your services to all beings.

Whatever your job is, dedicate it to others, that they may attain happiness.

IF YOU CAN'T THINK OF BENEFITING *all* beings, at least think of those few who will derive any kind of comfort from your effort, from your precious time and energy. Consider their happiness. And, from time to time as you do your work, as you go about your job, pause to reflect in this way, to rededicate your efforts. No matter what work you do, even if you don't like your job, keep the thought of others in your heart; the work will be the same, but your attitude will be different.

This is how you integrate work and meditation so that work itself becomes meditation.

Do your work with the good heart.

WHETHER YOU WORK in a Dharma cen-
ter, at home, or anywhere else, your attitude
should be that you are there for other beings to
make use of. When you don't have this attitude
of sacrificing yourself for others, if you believe
you should be the master and other beings your
servants, your work becomes a problem. When
you have this attitude, your work becomes a
pleasure—even though it is the same. When
you change your attitude so that beings are the
masters and you their servant, the problem is
stopped, and there is only enjoyment. Then,
no matter how hard the work is, and even if
you don't succeed in it, you enjoy it.

Love

If you want to be loved, love others first.

WHEN YOU TAKE CARE of your mind, when you hold your mind in a state of patience, of wisdom, or of compassion, only then are you truly loving yourself, only then are you really protecting yourself.

WITHOUT UNDERSTANDING the nature of mind and the working of karma, there is no way you can love yourself. You first have to correctly understand the evolution of happiness and suffering; otherwise, you may think you are loving yourself when you are actually harming yourself. This is what is happening often, perhaps even most of the time!

As His Holiness the Dalai Lama often says, the best way to love yourself is to cherish others; the only practical way to be "selfish" is to cherish other beings.

Less desire means more freedom. As desire lessens, the space for genuine love expands.

ROMANTIC OBSESSION is different from sincere love. In becoming romantically obsessed, you hallucinate about the person you desire and maybe that person hallucinates about you too. But it's important to try not to be caught up in that hallucinated view, and to look at the person with a different view, the view of wisdom and compassion.

Examine your motivation carefully!

IF YOU HAVE NO POSITIVE motivation of
benefiting beings and no motivation of renunciation, and instead if your relationship
(whether real or wished-for) is motivated by
self-cherishing thought, attachment, and desire,
then, as you get closer to your object of attachment, the object that you hallucinatingly
believe will dispel all suffering, you are really
getting closer to the hells.

SINCERE LOVE, on the other hand, means
love without any expectation that the other
person will want you, or be nice to you, or do
anything at all for you in return. Sincere love
means helping someone out of loving-kindness
and compassion, simply because that person
is suffering and you wish him or her to be
free from suffering and to be happy. Whether

people thank you or not, you help them because they have a problem and need help. That is the essence of sincere love.

You are never alone: everywhere, all the time there are numberless buddhas and bodhisattvas surrounding you, loving you, guiding you—after all, that is what they do.

WHEN IT COMES TIME for a relationship to end, or even if your partner leaves you for another person, you can begin to transform some of your suffering by thinking like this: "Since I enjoyed being with my partner, why shouldn't someone else have the same enjoyment? That other person is just as important as I am. Just like me, that person wants happiness and doesn't want suffering."

LOVING YOURSELF IS FINE, but it doesn't work if the method isn't right. The best way to really love yourself is to renounce each self-cherishing thought.

·   *Ignorance*   ·

LIVING IN IGNORANCE IS LIKE living in
a solid iron box, a prison more frightening and
inescapable than any earthly prison. But when
you practice renouncing attachment, when you
stop clinging to this life, to future lives, and to
samsaric happiness, when you cultivate compassion and awareness of the emptiness of all
phenomena, you are free. When you do this,
no prison will ever truly hold you.

**If you don't defeat your delusion,
no other victory is real.**

The creator of samsara is ignorance.

OUR MIND CREATES PROBLEMS when we believe something that isn't true, something that contradicts reality. When our expectations, which are contradictory to the reality of these phenomena, aren't met, a neutral phenomenon becomes a problem.

Where there is hallucination, there can be found truth, by recognizing it as hallucination.

LOOK AT THE REALITY of self, action, object; friend, enemy, stranger; your own body; your possessions, friends, and relatives. All these phenomena are transitory in nature, changing within every second due to various causes and conditions. Not only that, but they can come to an end at any time. This is the nature of all phenomena.

Yet, while these things are transitory in nature, we look at them as permanent. We see a permanent friend, permanent enemy, permanent possessions, permanent body, permanent life, permanent mind. We apprehend impermanent things to be permanent. That is a fundamental problem.

Where there is suffering, there can be found bliss, by electing to experience it for all beings.

WITH THE WRONG CONCEPTIONS of permanence and true existence, we apprehend things to be permanent and truly existent, and believe in those hallucinations—this is the nature of ignorance.

THINGS DO NOT EXIST INDEPENDENTLY but in dependence upon causes and conditions. Even ignorance is not independent; it too is a dependent arising.

**Believing your hallucinations
is the foundation of every harmful
thought, word, and deed.**

WHEN A TABLE IS COVERED with a table-cloth, we can't see what it is actually made of. Similarly, a layer of hallucination covers the collection of causes and conditions we label "I"—body and mind, the merely labeled senses, the merely labeled sense objects. Believing our hallucination, our label, we can't see past it to the true nature of the self.

IGNORANCE IS NOT WHAT SCIENTISTS might call "instinct." Ignorance is not spontaneously born from its own side; it's something that we create. We create ignorance each time we believe in the appearance of things as existing from their own side, as not being merely labeled. This ignorance is the basis of all delusions, of all karma, and of all suffering.

The concept of true existence is completely unnecessary.

THIS IS AN IMPORTANT POINT: the thought that labels "I" in dependence upon the aggregates is *not* the ignorance that is the root of samsara. That thought is not "wrong." When the *I* appears to you, it appears to have true existence from its own side, to be the complete opposite of being merely labeled, merely imputed. But the mind to which the truly existent *I* appears is *still* not the root of samsara. The root of samsara is the thought that believes, "This truly existent *I* that appears to me is true." This is the concept of true existence, and *this* is the root of samsara. This is the container of all problems.

Ignorance of the true nature of the "I" is more harmful than a million atomic bombs.

Karma

HAPPINESS AND SUFFERING have to do with your own virtuous and nonvirtuous actions, your positive and negative karma. Karma is your own thought; it is the intentions of your own mind.

WHENEVER YOU FOLLOW the arising of a nonvirtuous thought, you shut yourself away into prison. Whenever you follow the arising of a virtuous thought, you throw open the gate to ultimate joy.

TRULY UNDERSTANDING the Buddha's teaching about karma will wake you from the incredible deep sleep of beginningless rebirth, of continual suffering, of life without choice, without control.

.

BY ABANDONING NEGATIVE KARMA, the actions that harm ourselves and all beings, we always have the freedom to abandon suffering. By abandoning negative karma, we free ourselves from the suffering of the past, and by purifying negative karma, we open ourselves to happiness now and in the future.

EVERY ACTION WE DO is like planting a seed; every action leaves an imprint on our mental continuum. When certain conditions come together, this imprint then manifests;

when conditions such as water, soil, and sunlight come together the seed comes to fruition as a sprout. Actions motivated by greed, anger, or self-cherishing come to fruition as problems in our life; the imprint manifests as suffering. Actions done out of love, nonattachment, and unselfishness come to fruition as happiness; the imprint manifests as freedom and joy.

IF YOU WANT TO HAVE APPLES from your garden, you have to plant the seed of an apple tree. In a similar way, if you generate the positive attitude of the good heart and live your life with this positive energy, you will do positive actions from which you will then experience peace and happiness, both temporary and ultimate. It's a natural process.

You can't expect to grow apples by planting corn or pumpkins or bananas.

NO MATTER HOW STRONG our igno-rance, anger, desire, self-cherishing, and other delusions are and no matter how much heavy negative karma we have created, these things are not permanent; all these obscurations are tem-porary. Like fog in the sky, the fog in the mind is not permanent; it will not always be there, it is not inherently part of the mind. Mental obscurations are phenomena that arise in accor-dance (or in *dependence,* we might say) upon causes and conditions, just like the fog that obscures the afternoon sun arises in accordance with the presence of heat and water and atmos-pheric conditions. Then, according to other causes, other atmospheric conditions, the fog lifts—and similarly, dependently upon such causes as creating positive karma and practicing mind-training, the inner fog can be blown away.

It is the same with a dirty cloth, or a dusty mirror. The dirt is temporary, not permanent. Dependently upon causes and conditions, the cloth becomes dirty, and dependently upon other causes and conditions, the cloth can become clean. In accordance with certain causes and conditions, a mirror can be covered by dust, so that it doesn't offer a clear reflection. But in accordance with other causes and conditions, the dust can be removed, so that the mirror can give a clear reflection.

There is always hope.

NO MATTER HOW BLACK WITH DIRT a cloth is, because it is not one with the dirt, it can always be cleaned. No matter how thick the dust on a mirror is, the mirror can always be cleaned. Like this, no matter how strong our delusions and how heavy the negative karma we have created, since our mind is not one with them, there is always hope; there is always the potential for our mind to be separated from these obscurations and become completely pure. You can be free from fear, guilt, and all other undesirable emotions. Your mind can become completely free from all faults and perfected in all realizations; your mind can become a fully enlightened mind, a buddha's mind.

DIFFERENT ACTIONS AND ATTITUDES have different effects on our mind. One way of acting obscures our mind; while another way of acting causes our mind to become free from obscurations and fully awakened. Doing an action with a negative attitude—with ignorance, anger, attachment, or another disturbed thought—obscures our mind. But when we live our life with non-hatred, non-attachment, non-ignorance, as well as the compassionate desire to benefit all beings, the ultimate effect is always positive.

NO MATTER HOW BADLY you have failed in your work or your spiritual practice up until now, and even if you have created the heaviest negative karma possible, this negative karma is only a causative phenomenon; it is not truly existent. And the one good quality that negative karma has is that it can be purified. There is always hope.

WHEN YOU MAKE A MOVIE, you record various images on a film. Afterward, when you put the film into a projector and turn on the electricity, the images on the film can be projected onto a screen. We experience karma in a similar way: all our actions, motivated by positive and negative impulses, are "recorded" as imprints on our mind-stream. At some point, sooner or later, circumstances in our life are such that this karmic "recording" gets played back, projected out. This is a cause of all our problems and all our happiness.

FROM REBIRTH UNTIL DEATH, everything—our own body, our senses, all the objects of our senses—is manifested, or projected, from an imprint left on our consciousness by our past karma. From rebirth until death, everything that appears to us in our daily life from morning until night has to do with our mind. All sense objects have to do with the view of our mind. When we go to a shop or a super-market, all the thousands of beautiful, ugly, and neutral things that we see have to do with our view, and our view is the projection of our mind. It is the same with everything else.

OUR BODY, OUR SENSES, the objects of our senses—everything we see is a projection of our mind. If our mind is impure, we see things as impure. If our mind is pure, we see things as pure. How we see things—as beauti-ful or ugly, as good or bad, friend or enemy—depends on how we look at them.

IF YOU HAVE DONE NOTHING to purify the imprint left by past negative karma, it will still be there and will eventually manifest as a problem.

However, we don't have to experience these problems. There is a solution. You need never experience these problems again.

Before a problem is experienced, we have the opportunity to purify its cause. By purifying the imprint left on our mind by actions done out of disturbing thoughts, we can become free of problems.

Purifying the cause solves the problem.

YOUR PAST IGNORANCE from beginningless time left imprints on your mental continuum, and this imprint is projected, like film from a film-projector. You see this projection as the concrete reality of the merely imputed *I.* That is a complete hallucination.

Labeling

**Don't let yourself be deceived
by your own mind.**

IMAGINE THAT AT DUSK you see a coiled
rope on the road. Because of the way the rope
is coiled and because it's dusk and you can't see
clearly, when you first see this form you label
it "snake." After you label it "snake," a snake
then appears to you. You're not aware that the
snake that appears to you is merely imputed by
your own mind because the snake doesn't
appear to you as merely imputed; it appears as
a "real" snake—independent, unlabeled, with
existence from its own side. But before you

apply the label "snake," there's no snake and no appearance of a snake. Only after you label "snake" and believe in your own label do you then see the appearance of a snake. However, if you were to look carefully and, say, shine a flashlight on it, then you would see very clearly that it is a rope, and you would recognize that to call it "a snake" is completely false.

Now relate this to the self, the *I*. You label "I" in dependence upon certain causes and conditions, the aggregates of body and mind. After the labeling of "I" is done, you believe in that and the *I* then appears to you—but when you shine the light of awareness, you see that this too is completely false.

Labeling a situation "bad" is not the problem; the problem comes when you start to believe in your own label.

BEFORE YOU LABEL "That is bad" upon some situation, there is no appearance of badness to you. Before you label "He doesn't like me" on another person's negative attitude toward you, there is not even the appearance to you of his disliking you. These appearances come from your own mind.

Believing your labels to be true is what makes life difficult.

When you label "He likes me" and believe that label, what you have labeled then appears to you. You label that person "friend," and because you believe your label, he appears to you as a friend. You label "enemy" on the person who is angry with you, and because you believe that label, he appears to you as an enemy. Both friend and enemy come from your own mind. "He likes me," "he doesn't like me," "she is helping me," "she is harming me"—all these come from your own mind. You interpret one action as help and another as harm; you label them, and they then appear as help or harm. Both come from your own mind.

One way to stop problems is to change your view of them, to stop believing your labels of problems as "bad."

THE PRACTICE OF RECOGNIZING labels as labels and not self-existent truths is itself also a practice of patience. Through simply being aware of the nature of your own thoughts and actions, you can begin to pacify your problems and obtain peace and happiness. Through

doing this, you start to find freedom within
your own mind.

**Hallucination covers the whole
of samsara *and* nirvana.
These too are merely labeled.**

ON ONE LABEL, another label is put; and
on that label, yet another one. From birth to
death, it's just like this.

Emptiness

EVERYTHING IS EMPTY from its own side. Ignorance of this is the cause of all suffering. Mindfulness of this gives liberation and enlightenment. It ceases all the faults of the mind.

Just as the *I* is completely empty, the aggregates to which the *I* is merely imputed are also completely empty.

OUR MIND MAKES UP an identity for the self; we project a self that is unlabeled and independent, a self that has nothing to do with its base, the association of body and mind, and nothing to do with the mind that labels it. We imagine there is something else, an unlabeled self with an existence from its own side—and we constantly try to protect this self. We are afraid that this real self will get into trouble or be unhappy or die.

Yet even though that real self doesn't exist from its own side at all, there *is* an I that sits, sleeps, eats, and walks, that experiences suffering and happiness, that looks for solutions to problems, that meditates, that seeks ultimate happiness. There is an I that does all these activities, but that I is nothing other than what is merely imputed by the mind to this base, this association of body and mind.

IN EMPTINESS THERE'S no "my mind" and "Buddha's mind"; there's no "emptiness of my mind" and "emptiness of Buddha's mind."

In emptiness, there's no this and that. Everything is of the same taste.

Look at everything—subject, action, object—as illusory.

EVERYTHING APPEARS TO US to be truly existent, unlabeled, but remember the reality is that there is not the slightest true existence. When we see a mirage, there is an appearance of water, but we understand that there's not even the slightest water there on the sand. Like this, everything—subject, action, object—appears to have existence from its own side, but you must understand that it is all a hallucination. In reality everything is empty.

Nothing has existence from its own side.

WITHOUT THE MIND THAT LABELS "I," there's no I. Without the mind that thinks of and labels the self, the self doesn't exist. Truly, the self is merely imputed to the association of body and mind by thought. From the I down to subatomic particles, everything is merely imputed, existing in mere name.

There is a big difference between reality and the projections that appear to us in our everyday life. Mistaking these two is the basis of all our other problems.

THE SELF IS NEITHER all aggregates together nor any any aggregate individually; nor does the self exist separately from the aggregates. If the *I* existed separately from the aggregates, even if the police put the body in prison, there would be no reason why the *I* would have to go to prison. Even if the body were sick, hungry, or thirsty, there would be no need for the *I* to be sick, hungry, or thirsty if it existed separately from the aggregates. And even if the mind were depressed, there would be no reason the *I* would have to be depressed. If the *I* existed separately from the aggregates, the *I* could go to Tibet and travel all over the world without the body (and we wouldn't need to worry about buying tickets or any other expenses!)—but, as you know, none of this is the case.

A thing exists in dependence upon causes and conditions, and that thing ceases to be when those causes and conditions cease to be.

CONSIDER THE CASE OF THE GRAINS we eat. When, due to certain causes and conditions, there are grains, then these grains can be used for food. When those grains are ground into powder, according to those causes and conditions, there is flour. Then, when the flour is made into noodles or a loaf of bread, due to those causes and conditions, there is bread or noodles. In this way, one phenomenon changes into different things at different times, due to different causes and conditions. First there is grain, then flour, then bread or noodles. And at the end, after it is eaten, it becomes excrement.

All the different phenomena that exist with these changes, with the different causes and conditions, are nothing other than what is merely imputed by the mind in dependence upon those changing bases. The different phenomena that exist during the gathering of those particular causes and conditions do not exist from their own side. They are merely imputed by the mind in dependence upon those bases, and we then believe in the existence of those different phenomena. Because of the different bases, we believe that there are these different phenomena.

None of these things called "grain," "flour," "dough," "bread," "noodles," and "excrement" exist from their own side. They are completely empty of existing from their own side because they are merely imputed by the mind in dependence upon those bases, those causes and conditions. From the grain down to the excrement, all those things are empty. But it's important to understand that these phenomena are not empty of *themselves*—the grain is not empty of grain—just empty of existing from their own side.

EVEN THOUGH THE *I* does not exist from its own side, it is also not nonexistent; the *I* can abandon the cause of suffering, create the cause of happiness, and do many things to benefit others.

We urgently need to realize emptiness. To wait even one second to do this is too long—it's like waiting for eons.

YOU CAN PRACTICE AWARENESS of emptiness in everyday life by meditating on dependent arising, looking at how everything—self, action, object—is merely imputed. Do this while you are working in the office, talking to people or having meetings, or while you are at home with your family. (But it's probably best not to do this while driving, for instance.) Do it especially when you are having a conversation with someone who is complaining about or criticizing you, which will cause the delu-sion of anger to arise, and when somebody is praising you, which will cause the delusion of pride to arise. Practice awareness of either dependent arising or emptiness. They're the same; it's one meditation.

Death

**If you don't remember death,
you don't remember the Dharma.**

THE GREAT BODHISATTVA Thogme
Zangpo, who composed *The Thirty-Seven Practices
of a Bodhisattva*, wrote a few verses of advice for
a practitioner who had asked how to practice
Dharma when facing illness or other problems:

> If your illusory body is sick, this is
> good. Why? Because just like doing var-
> ious spiritual practices, this illness will
> purify obscurations.
>
> If you don't have any disease, this is

also good. Why? Because the purpose of having a healthy body and mind is to make your human life meaningful.

If you are poor, this is good. Why? Because you don't have to worry about losing or protecting your wealth or about competing with others. All quarrels and fighting come from clinging to material possessions; if you don't have possessions, there is nothing to cling to or fight about.

If you are wealthy, this is good. Why? Because you can accumulate more merit, which leads to temporary and ultimate happiness. All good fortune is definitely the result of good karma, or merit.

If you are going to die soon, this is good. Why? Because with the help of positive imprints, you can definitely enter the unmistaken path without obstacles such as disease.

If you are not going to die soon but will live long, this is good. Why? Since you have received the instructions, which are like water, minerals, and heat, by practicing while you have the opportunity, you can ripen your mind and grow the crop of realizations.

In every *second* of this human life you have the freedom to choose between hell and enlightenment, samsara and liberation.

NO MATTER WHAT HAPPENS in your life, transform your mind into happiness. Whether you are sick or healthy, poor or rich, dying soon or living long, make it meaningful by trying to benefit others.

WE MISTAKENLY BELIEVE that there are some phenomena that are permanent. When we look at each moment of time, we think it will somehow last forever. We think the same thing about the self, our body, our possessions, the people around us, the whole world. We cling feverishly to these beliefs, until suddenly we find that it's not true. Then, when death or loss come as they inevitably will, unexpectedly seeing the reality of impermanence brings us all kinds of suffering: shock, fear, depression, nervous breakdowns. But permanence is just a hallucination. The more deeply we understand that, the less we are disturbed to find that it is true.

Death can always come in the next minute. Make sure you practice Dharma right now.

WHEN IT FINALLY COMES TIME for you to die, or even if you have a strong fear of death, use that as an opportunity to practice the path. Think to yourself: "There are numberless beings who have already died, who are dying today, and who will die in the future. How wonderful it would be if I could experience all that suffering by myself alone, enabling them to be free of that suffering. Therefore, I am going to experience my death on behalf of all other beings." In this way, you are using your death on the path to enlightenment. And in this way, you can contemplate your death and even actually *die* with a happy mind.

Every moment of this human life is more precious than skies of jewels. Please appreciate it.

Meditations

The sun of real happiness shines in your life
when you start to cherish others.

LAMA ZOPA RINPOCHE is one of the most internationally renowned masters of Tibetan Buddhism, working and teaching ceaselessly on almost every continent.

He is the spiritual director and co-founder of the Foundation for the Preservation of the Mahayana Tradition (FPMT), an international network of Buddhist projects, including monasteries in six countries and meditation centers in over thirty; health and nutrition clinics, and clinics specializing in the treatment of leprosy and polio; as well as hospices, schools, publishing activities, and prison outreach projects worldwide.

Lama Zopa Rinpoche is the author of numerous books, including *Transforming Problems into Happiness, Ultimate Healing,* and *Dear Lama Zopa.*

May I always support the lives
Of all the boundless creatures.

With this verse we are requesting to become the basis, the support, the very life-foundation of all the inconceivably vast number of beings—and not just briefly, for a moment or two or a few days, but forever. When we give away our bodies in this fashion, it is up to those other beings to decide how to use the elements of our bodies—the earth, water, fire, air, and space—for their happiness. It's not up to the elements to decide; it's not up to us.

To do this practice, imagine the following: First imagine that the four elements that form your own body absorb into the four external elements of earth, water, fire, and air. Imagine that your flesh and bones absorb into the external earth element. Imagine that your body becomes the stable earth and is used by all beings in whatever way they wish for their survival and happiness, not only in this world but in all worlds.

· *Giving Your Body Away* ·

This is a short meditation on thought transformation, in which we dedicate the four elements of our bodies to the happiness of all beings, putting into practice the action of renouncing self and cherishing others.

HIS HOLINESS THE DALAI LAMA often quotes the following verse from Shantideva's *A Guide to the Bodhisattva's Way of Life*:

> Just like space
> And the great elements such as earth
> [and water, fire, and air],

You can conclude *tonglen* by meditating for a little while on the emptiness of the I, maintaining awareness that the I is empty of existing from its own side.

thing—all your own happiness and merit, the causes of happiness; your own body; your possessions—to the hell beings, hungry ghosts, animals, humans, and the beings enjoying the heavens. Your body becomes a wish-granting jewel and you offer charity to all beings. All their environments become pure realms.

Clearly envision that those who need money receive wealth—each person owns the whole sky filled with money. Those who need a guru find a perfectly qualified teacher who can reveal the whole path to enlightenment to them. Those who need medicine receive it. Those who need a doctor, or a husband, or a wife, or a friend, find one. Each being receives whatever is needed for happiness.

Through this practice, all beings receive whatever they need, and all these enjoyments become the cause only to purify their minds and to generate in their minds the path to ultimate happiness, so that they all become fully enlightened beings. Imagine they all become Chenrezig—the Buddha of Compassion.

nostrils and let it be completely absorbed into the self-cherishing thought at your heart, completely destroying that self-cherishing thought with each breath.

Remember: It is your self-cherishing thought that interferes all the time with your immediate and ultimate happiness and with your ability to free all beings from all their sufferings and obscurations and to lead them to immediate and ultimate happiness.

As you breathe in this smoke and absorb it into your self-cherishing thought, the self-cherishing thought starts to become nonexistent. As the self-cherishing thought becomes nonexistent, so does the "real" I, the I existing from its own side, which the self-cherishing thought regards as so precious and important. Just as the self-cherishing thought becomes nonexistent, so does the object it cherishes.

All that is left there is what is merely imputed. This merely imputed *I* then breathes out happiness, and freedom, and light—and offers charity to other beings. The merely imputed *I* breathes out and offers every-

· *Taking and Giving* ·

There is an important meditation practice called tonglen, *which means "taking and giving." It is the practice of "taking" all the suffering of all beings, transforming it, and "giving" joy and happiness to all beings. You can also use this practice to free yourself from your self-cherishing thought, to utterly destroy the self-cherishing thought. Here are some basic instructions.*

IMAGINE BREATHING in a thick black smoke. Imagine that this smoke is all the suffering of the world, all the harm that comes to all beings, all the pain and sickness everywhere. Also breathe in all the undesirable environments experienced by humans, animals, hungry ghosts, and the many suffering beings in the hell realms. Imagine breathing this in through your

To find out more about the FPMT, contact:
FPMT Interinational Office
1632 SE 11th Avenue
Portland, OR 97214-4702 USA
Tel. 503-808-1588 | Fax 503-808-1589
www.fpmt.org

THE LAMA YESHE WISDOM ARCHIVES

The Lama Yeshe Wisdom Archive (LYWA) houses an archival collection of the teachings of Lama Zopa Rinpoche and his teacher, Lama Thubten Yeshe. To find out more, contact:

LYWA
PO Box 356
Weston, MA 02493 USA
Tel. 781-259-4466 | www.lamayeshe.org

About Wisdom

WISDOM PUBLICATIONS, a nonprofit publisher, is dedicated to making available authentic works relating to Buddhism for the benefit of all. To learn more about Wisdom, or to browse books online or request a catalog, we invite you to visit our website at www.wisdompubs.org.

THE WISDOM TRUST

As a nonprofit publisher, Wisdom is dependent in part upon the kindness and generosity of sponsors in order to fulfill our publishing mission. If you would like to make a donation to Wisdom, you may do so through our website or our Somerville office. If you would like to help sponsor the publication of a book, please contact us at info@wisdompubs.org or the address on the copyright page of this book. Thank you.

Wisdom is a nonprofit, charitable 501(c)(3) organization affiliated with the Foundation for the Preservation of the Mahayana Tradition (FPMT).

Imagine that your body is used by all beings as fields and crops; beautiful parks, roads, and vehicles; to obtain gold, diamonds, and other precious jewels; to build houses and cities; to make tunnels and bridges. Visualize this as elaborately as possible.

Your two eyes then become the sun and moon and work for all beings, illuminating them, guiding them. Your flesh becomes food for all beings. Visualize that your flesh absorbs into all the food in the world, all the food in all the supermarkets. You become pizzas, mozzarella cheese, macaroni, hamburgers, *momos*—and all beings everywhere are eating you. Again, it is important to think of not just one being in this world, but of all beings in every world. Give your skin to all beings—let your skin become the clothes that beings are wearing, or the hair or fur or feathers that keep them warm.

Visualize the blood, water, and other liquids in your body absorbing into the external water element, which is also used by all beings for their survival and happiness. Think of the many different ways in which the water of the world, which is none other than your own body's fluids, is used by beings for their happiness. Again, visualize as extensively as possible the many different uses of water—it floods rice paddies, it flows through irrigation canals, it nourishes flowers, it appears as nectar, it quenches thirst everywhere. Beings are drinking you as orange juice, Coca-Cola, alcohol, mother's milk, Gatorade.

Next, imagine that the internal heat of your body absorbs into the external fire element, which is used by all beings for their happiness. Think of how heat and the ability to burn benefit all beings—heat keeps them warm, it gives them light, it creates energy; heat is used for cooking and survival, for safety and exploration. As always, imagine this as extensively as possible, in as much detail as possible.

Your breath absorbs into the external air, the wind element, which is used by all beings for their survival through breathing and moving. Wind is light in nature and enables movement, grants freedom. Breath is life itself. Let yourself be breathed in by all beings, bringing life-sustaining oxygen to every cell in the body of every being.

Now imagine that all the sufferings and negative karmas of all beings everywhere ripen upon you—and thereby know that all beings are freed from all their suffering and its causes, all their negative karmas and obscurations.

Let all the harmful karma of all beings everywhere come to fruition, and let yourself receive all the results. Absorb all this suffering and all its causes into your own self-cherishing thought, destroying that thought and the object it cherishes, the "real" I. Now even the real I, which appears to exist from its own side, becomes empty.

All that is left is the merely imputed I, and this one now dedicates all your happiness and merit to all beings. All the beings in each realm receive and experience your past, present, and future happiness and merit. In the same way, also dedicate all the merit of the buddhas and bodhisattvas throughout space and time. Know that this merit is also received and experienced by all beings.

In this way, your body, composed of the four elements, becomes nectar—and into this nectar of your body flows the transcendental wisdom from the hearts of all the buddhas and bodhisattvas. The essence of all the worlds is also absorbed into the nectar. And this nectar nourishes and supports all beings, immediately fulfilling all their wishes, giving them ultimate happiness, ultimate joy.

And now, since you have offered your body to all beings of the six realms, it no longer exists. All that is left now is your mind, which doesn't have natural existence, which doesn't exist from its own side. Focus on its actual nature, its emptiness. Bring to awareness the fact that the mind doesn't have the slightest existence from its own side, that it's completely empty.

Now recite OM AH HUM seven times.

Then dedicate the merit.

· *Dedicating Merit* ·

The best way to dedicate merit is to dedicate it to achieve enlight-enment for all beings. When you do this, that merit becomes inex-haustible, unceasing. A very important point when you dedicate merit is to also dedicate it in the purest way, by "sealing it with emptiness." By specifically concentrating on the meaning of "mere imputation," the emptiness of all things from their own side, you make your dedication in a way that is pure and unstained by the concept of true existence. Doing this, sealing your dedication with emptiness, renders it indestructible—it will never be destroyed by any future greed, anger, or wrong views. Sealing the dedication with emptiness gives great protection, like storing your money or possessions in an uncrackable, disaster-proof safe.

To dedicate merit, think to yourself:

> DUE TO THE MERITS of the three times—past, present, and future—accumulated by me and by all other beings, may *bodhichitta*, the good heart, the source of all happiness and success, be generated in my own mind and in the minds of all other beings. May those who have already generated *bodhichitta* increase it.

And then, to seal the dedication with empti-ness, think to yourself:

DUE TO ALL THE MERITS of the three times, which are merely imputed, accumulated by me and by all other be-ings, which are merely imputed, may the *I*, which is merely imputed, achieve enlightenment, which is merely impu-ted, and lead all beings, who are merely imputed, to enlightenment, which is merely imputed.